11/00

Native Americans

The Iroquois

Richard M. Gaines

ABDO Publishing Company

visit us at
www.abdopub.com

Published by ABDO Publishing Company, 4940 Viking Drive, Suite 622, Edina, Minnesota 55435. Copyright © 2000 Abdo Consulting Group, Inc., Pentagon Tower, P.O. Box 36036, Minneapolis, Minnesota 55435 USA. International copyrights reserved in all countries. No part of this book may be reproduced in any form without written permission from the publisher.

Printed in the United States.

Illustrators: John Fadden (pgs. 7, 9, 11, 12, 15, 17, 19, 23, 24, 25, 27); Barbara Gray (pgs. 18, 21, 23)
Cover photo of Tuscaroran bonnet courtesy of the Smithsonian Institution
Interior Photos: Sally M. K. Benedict (pgs. 8, 28, 29, 30)—longhouse photos on page 8 were taken at Droulers/
           Tsiionhiakwatha archaeological site in Akwesasne Mohawk Territory
           Barbara Gray (pgs. 12, 13, 14, 20)
           Corbis (pg. 22)
Editors: Bob Italia, Tamara L. Britton, Kate A. Furlong
Art Direction & Maps: Pat Laurel
Border Design: Barbara Gray; Carey Molter/MacLean & Tuminelly (Mpls.)

Library of Congress Cataloging-in-Publication Data

Gaines, Richard M., 1942-
   The Iroquois / Richard M. Gaines
     p. cm. -- (Native Americans)
   Includes bibliographical references and index.
   Summary: Presents a brief introduction to the Iroquois Indians including information on their society, homes, food, clothing, crafts, and life today.
   ISBN 1-57765-373-4
   1. Iroquois Indians--Juvenile literature. [1. Iroquois Indians. 2. Indians of North America.] I. Title.

E99.I7 G35 2000
974. 7'0049755--dc21

99-059869

ON THE COVER: The border has special meaning to the Iroquois. The turtles represent Mother Earth. The blue half-circles represent the celestial sky, from which the Iroquois came. The swirl on the top represents the celestial tree, which was uprooted and formed the hole that Sky Woman fell through. The small yellow symbol beneath the celestial sky represents corn, which was important to Iroquois survival.

Contributing Editor: Barbara Gray, JD

Barbara Gray, JD (Kanatiyosh) is a member of the Mohawk Nation (Akwesasne), which is in New York State and Canada. Barbara earned her Juris Doctorate from Arizona State University College of Law in May of 1999. She is presently pursuing a Doctorate in Justice Studies that focuses on American Indian culture and issues at Arizona State University. When she finishes school, she will return home to the Mohawk Nation.

Contents

Homeland

The original Iroquois homelands covered a large area of North America. The Iroquois lived in parts of present-day Ohio, Pennsylvania, New York, Quebec, and Ontario.

Forests of maple, beech, elm, ash, oak, chestnut, birch, pine, and hemlock trees covered their land. The woods were home to deer, bear, turkey, rabbit, squirrel, beaver, and porcupine. Millions of passenger pigeons arrived in March to nest in the trees.

Many streams and rivers flowed into the lakes, especially Lake Ontario. They contained trout, pike, perch, bass, salmon, turtles, and eels. **Migrating** swans, geese, and ducks rested in the lakes.

Plenty of rain fell on the Iroquois' land. In the winter, there were heavy snowstorms.

Today, the Iroquois have **reservations** in New York, Quebec, and Ontario. There are also Iroquois reservations in Wisconsin and Oklahoma.

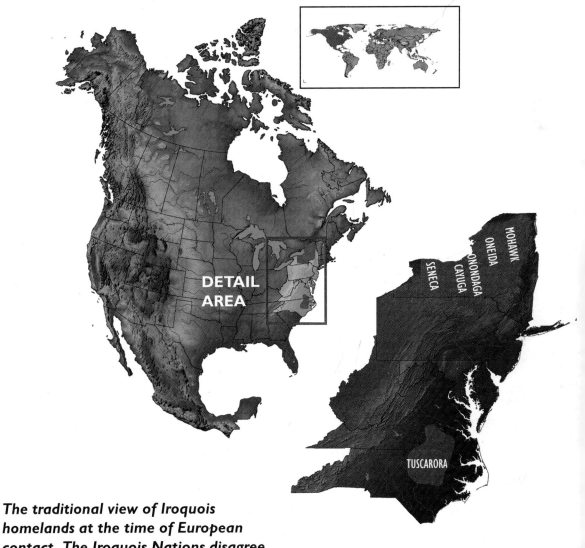

DETAIL AREA

MOHAWK
ONEIDA
ONONDAGA
CAYUGA
SENECA

TUSCARORA

The traditional view of Iroquois homelands at the time of European contact. The Iroquois Nations disagree with this view, and are still discussing land rights with the U.S. government.

5

Society

The original five Iroquois nations were the Mohawk, Oneida, Onondaga, Cayuga, and Seneca. They formed an **alliance** called the Haudenosaunee (ho-dee-no-SHO-nee). It means the "People of the Longhouse." The English called this alliance the Five Nations or the Iroquois **Confederacy**.

Later, relatives of these nations fled North Carolina. They were called the Tuscarora. They traveled to New York and joined the Haudenosaunee. The five nations became six nations strong.

The Iroquois lived in villages. Each **clan** lived in a longhouse, the **traditional**-style home of the Iroquois.

DEER BEAR HERON EEL BEAVER SNIPE TURTLE WOLF HAWK

The nine clans of the Haudenosaunee

Clans were named after animals. A **clan symbol** was painted above each longhouse door. The symbol identified the family inside. Bear, Turtle, and Wolf are Mohawk clans. Clans are passed down from mother to child.

Today, 50 chiefs and **49 clan mothers** lead the Haudenosaunee. This Grand Council makes important decisions for the Confederacy and their individual nations. For over 500 years, the Haudenosaunee has kept peace among the Iroquois nations.

A leader of the Seneca Nation holds a unity wampum belt as he talks peace with a group of Algonquin.

Homes

A longhouse frame

A finished longhouse

Longhouse platforms

To make a longhouse, the Iroquois used four big elm posts. These posts formed the frame's four corners. Then, young elm trees were cut and tied into place. They formed the frame's sides and rounded roof.

The Iroquois covered the longhouse frames with elm bark. Strips of bark were carefully cut and pressed flat with rocks. Then, the elm-bark siding was tied together with rope. The rope was made from the inner bark of the slippery elm tree.

Inside the longhouse, each family had its own living area. Each living area had a cooking pit with a **smoke hole** in the ceiling.

An Iroquois clan listens to a storyteller inside a longhouse.

The Iroquois slept on platforms. In the poles above their platforms, they hung and stored items like corn. Under the platforms, they stored dried beans and squash in big clay pots.

Food

The Iroquois farmed, hunted, and fished. They also gathered food that grew naturally. Each spring, women planted corn, beans, and squash. These crops are known as the "Three Sisters." That's because they grow from Mother Earth.

The Iroquois planted crops in community gardens near the village walls. The gardens were tended through the summer. The crops were harvested in September or October. Women and children also collected wild roots, berries, plums, cherries, and nuts.

Iroquois men hunted all year. They shot deer with bows and arrows. They trapped bear and beaver. They **snared** rabbits, ducks, and geese.

Iroquois families traveled to the streams and lakes to catch fish. They made fishing lines and nets from twisted plant fibers. They made hooks from bird and fish bones.

The Iroquois dried most of the fish. They hung them in the **rafters** above the longhouse platforms.

Early 20th century Iroquois harvesting corn using hand scythes, back burden baskets, and stacking stalks in "kaheroton" (teepee shapes). The woman sitting on the low stool is putting corn into braids.

Clothing

Beadwork in woodland design

The Iroquois made clothing from natural materials. They used furs, and elk and deer **hides**. And they wove fabric from corn husks and plant fibers.

Iroquois women wore deerskin dresses, or a long deerskin blouse with a skirt. Women also wore knee-high leggings and moccasins.

Women decorated their clothing with porcupine **quills**. Today, they also use glass seed beads to create **woodland designs**.

A man, woman, and young boy wearing traditional Iroquois clothing. The man is wearing a gustoweh. Its three upright feathers identify him as a Mohawk. The young boy is holding a lacrosse stick.

Men wore a tanned leather breechcloth. It hung down in front and back. And they wore leggings.

Men also wore fringed deerskin shirts and **hide** moccasins. These were decorated with a **woodland design**. Men and women had winter robes of bear, buffalo, or elk hides.

Iroquois men wore a special hat called a gustoweh. It was made from curved wood splints. The hat was covered with split feathers. The number of eagle feathers on the top of the hat told what Iroquois nation the man was from. Men's jewelry was made of bear's teeth and claws, and beads made of shell or carved bone.

Chief Joseph Mitchell (1976 Turtle Clan) wearing a gustoweh

Children wore clothes similar to the adults. Babies wore diapers made from the fat end of a **cattail**.

Today, the clothing style is the same. The Iroquois still use leather. And men still wear gustowehs. But cotton is also used for shirts and dresses.

Crafts

The Iroquois wove cornhusks together to make rugs, sleeping mats, sandals, and dolls for children. The Iroquois used **wampum** to record history and for trade.

Wampum shell and beads

The Iroquois traded with the Native Americans that lived close to the ocean to get seashells needed to make wampum. The Iroquois made purple wampum beads from the Quahog clamshell. They made white beads from the center part of the **Atlantic whelk**.

Wampum beads are strung on strings. Each Iroquois Nation is represented by different combinations of wampum bead colors. Wampum beads are also woven into belts with symbols that tell Iroquois history.

A Two-Row Wampum belt

One **wampum** belt is known as the "Two-Row Wampum." It has two rows of purple wampum beads. Rows of white wampum run on the sides of the purple rows. One purple row stands for the white man's laws. The other row of purple stands for Iroquois laws.

The belt shows that there are two different sets of laws. It also shows that Iroquois law is for the Iroquois people, and that neither group should block the other's law.

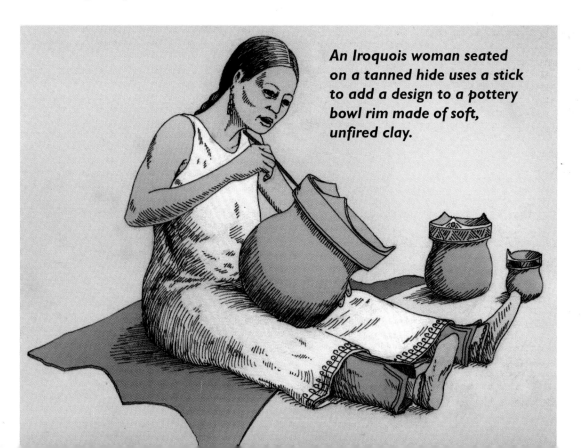

An Iroquois woman seated on a tanned hide uses a stick to add a design to a pottery bowl rim made of soft, unfired clay.

Family

The **clan mothers** were responsible for approving marriages. Clan members could not marry a person from the same clan.

The mothers of the couple who wanted to get married had to agree that the marriage was good. If the mothers did not agree, then the couple could not be married. The Iroquois respected their mothers' decisions.

If the couple was married, the son would leave his mother's longhouse. The longhouse of his wife's family became his new home.

Girls learned from their mothers and relatives how to sew, gather food, and how to plant crops. Young girls also learned by playing with cornhusk dolls. And they learned by watching nature.

Fathers taught their sons how to make arrowheads. They showed them how to hunt, fish, and trade. They also taught them how to defend themselves if they ran into trouble.

All children had to learn the nation's songs and dances. And they had to learn how to use medicine plants.

Early in the morning, women hung a clay pot filled with soup over the fire. Iroquois families ate one main meal. Often, it was taken in the middle of the day.

An Iroquois woman prepares corn in a corn pounder. The corn is being pounded into flour. The Iroquois grew at least thirteen kinds of corn, including popcorn.

Children

Iroquois babies were born in the longhouse. They were given a bath, then wrapped in soft **pelts**.

Within a few days, the new mother returned to her daily jobs. The baby was bundled up and gently tied into a **cradleboard**. The mother carried the cradleboard on her back. Or she could lean it against a tree next to her as she worked.

Cradleboards had a protective wooden band in front of the baby's head. If the cradleboard fell, the band would protect the baby from injury. Iroquois carved and painted cradleboards with **woodland designs** and their clan animal.

Iroquois children were taught to respect their parents, elders, and the entire natural world. Iroquois parents never struck their children.

A birchbark painting of an Iroquois boy playing with a javelin. In one form of the game, the object was to throw the javelin through center of the rolling hoop.

Children usually obeyed their parents and behaved well. When they misbehaved, their parents would talk to them. If that did not work, they sprayed a mouthful of water on the children. Sometimes adults told scary tales to teach the children how to act properly.

Iroquois children loved to play games. A popular game was called javelin. It was played with a hickory stick and wooden hoop.

An older Iroquois woman and her daughter, who is holding a baby in cradleboard. Behind them is the arched "skydome." Within it is the moon with the image of a wolf's head. The wolf image is also on the cradleboard tie. All three Iroquois belong to the Wolf Clan, which follows through the mother. The Iroquois consider the moon as their "Grandmother."

Sky Woman

The Iroquois used **myths** to explain many things about life. The Sky Woman myth explained the creation of the Earth.

§

Long ago, Sky Woman fell through the hole in the sky. She entered a world of water and darkness where animal spirits lived.

A flock of geese-like spirits saw Sky Woman falling. They caught her on their wings. The geese placed Sky Woman on the back of the Great Turtle. Then the animal spirits dove for mud on the ocean floor.

An Iroquois water drum

The muskrat died while trying to gather the mud. But the beaver found mud in muskrat's little paws and mouth.

The beaver handed the mud to Sky Woman. She placed it on the Great Turtle's back. Then Sky Woman took a **water drum**

20

out of her pouch. She began to dance and sing. As she danced, the Great Turtle began to grow.

This is how Sky Woman brought Turtle Island (North America) into existence. Today, when there is an earthquake, the Iroquois tell their children not to be afraid. The Great Turtle is just stretching.

A birchbark painting of Sky Woman with a water drum, standing on the back of the Great Turtle

War

The word "Iroquois" means "real **adders**." The Algonquin gave this name to the Haudenosaunee during a time of conflict.

The Iroquois were respected for their ability to outwit their enemies. They used wooden bows and arrows, knives, and clubs. Arrowheads were made of flint. Knives were made from animal leg bones. War clubs were made of stone, wood, or deer antlers.

An Iroquois war club

The wooden-ball war club had a carved handle and a wooden ball head. The war club worked well in close combat. It could also be thrown.

Going to war was not taken lightly. Everyone had to agree that the only solution to a problem was to fight. Once everyone agreed to fight, a war club was hung on the war post. The club was painted red. Black **wampum** was attached to it. This meant that the **clans** had agreed to go to war.

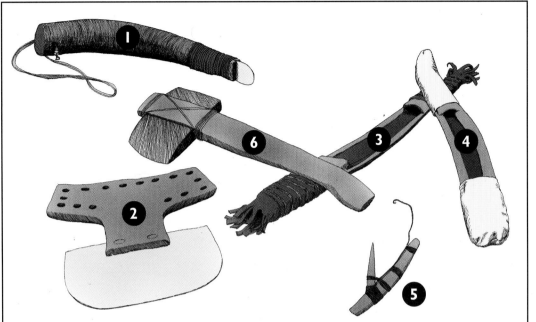

The Iroquois used bows and arrows, knives, and clubs in war. Sometimes, they also used tools as weapons. Some tools that they used were metal hide scrapers (1) and (2), and bone and leather hide scrapers (3) and (4). Fish hooks (5) and stone axes (6) were used, too.

The border on the right shows weapons beneath the Tree of Peace. The Iroquois buried their weapons long ago when they adopted the Peacemaker's Great Law of Peace. Leaders of the Iroquois nations decided only to fight when protecting their peoples and preserving their land for future generations.

Contact with Europeans

When the European explorers first met the Iroquois, they were surprised at how well built the Iroquois villages were.

In 1535, Jacques Cartier came upon the village of Hochelaga near present-day Montreal. This huge Iroquois town had a wooden wall that surrounded the village of longhouses. It was 18 feet (5 m) high. More than three thousand people lived inside.

Behind the wall were platforms. The Iroquois could stand on the platforms, look over the wall, and spot approaching enemies. The platforms also provided a place for them to hurl stones or shoot arrows at enemies. Some Europeans called these Iroquois villages "castles" because they were so well protected.

Life inside Hochelaga: The man with the bow and the two young boys is returning from an unsuccessful hunt. The woman near the longhouse is grinding corn. The little building on stilts is for corn storage. The Turtle Clan symbol is on the animal skin covering the door where the chief is sitting.

In 1609, French explorer Samuel Champlain and his Algonquin guides traveled into Iroquois lands. When they met the Iroquois, a battle began. The French killed the Iroquois chiefs with their guns. The Iroquois had never seen guns before.

The Peacemaker

The Peacemaker was a great **prophet** and lawgiver. He was from the Huron tribe. He knew as a child that war only wasted lives and caused suffering.

As an adult, the Peacemaker and Hiawatha (*Aiionwatha*) began a journey. They wanted to spread the message of peace.

Soon, they reached the land of the Mohawks. During the Peacemaker's time, the Mohawk, Oneida, Onondaga, Cayuga, and Seneca were always at war with each other. The Peacemaker told the Mohawks that he had been sent with a message of peace. The Mohawks wanted him to prove it.

The Peacemaker said he would climb into a tree along the Mohawk River. Once in the tree, the Mohawks should cut it down. The Peacemaker would fall into the dangerous river rapids. But he said he would return.

The Peacemaker climbed into the tree. The Mohawks chopped it down. Then, the Peacemaker fell into the rapids.

The next morning, the Mohawks found the Peacemaker sitting by their fire, as he had promised. They listened to his message and accepted the **Great Law of Peace**.

The Peacemaker in a stone canoe. On the distant shore stand his mother and grandmother. The symbol on his shirt represents growing plants.

The Iroquois Today

In 1995, there were 74,882 Iroquois living in North America. More than 17,118 lived on **reservations** in New York. Another 35,624 lived on reservations in Ontario, Canada. There were 9,631 Iroquois living in reservations in Quebec, Canada. Over 10,000 Iroquois lived in Wisconsin, and 2,000 in Oklahoma.

The Iroquois no longer live in longhouses. But they use them for ceremonies. Today's longhouses are built from modern wood boards. They are still long, and have only two doors.

A Mohawk child wearing contemporary traditional Mohawk clothing

Grand Chief Michael Kanentakeron and his uncle Louis Mitchell stand in front of the wooden carving of Saiowisakeron John Ice Fire, a Mohawk patriot.

Some of today's longhouses are built of wood boards.

A Mohawk quiltmaker displays one of her beautiful quilts.

Some Iroquois people may have forgotten some of the **traditional** ways. Some may not know much about their culture. Some reservations have suffered because industry has polluted their lands.

But many Iroquois people still follow the Peacemaker's traditional teachings. They are cleaning up the environment, and preserving their culture.

Akwesasne Mohawks in pow-wow style costuming (Photo by Daniel W. George)

A Kawehnoke day Care Center teacher with a young Mohawk student

Young Iroquois in traditional dress doing the rabbit dance (Photo by Daniel W. George)

Harvesting sap for maple syrup (Photo by Daniel W. George)

Traditional Mohawk Chief Jake Swamp, award-winning author

Today, Iroquois people hold many types of jobs. Many Iroquois have become doctors, lawyers, and teachers. Many men still do steelwork on high-rise structures, for which they have become famous. But there are still chiefs, **clan mothers**, and **faithkeepers**. It is their duty to protect the environment for future generations.

Akwesasne Mohawk Paralegal class at the Supreme Court of Canada

Mohawk elders Florence Katsitsienhawi Benedict, a famous basketmaker and quilter, and Dr. Ernest Kaientaronkwen Benedict, a nationally respected educator

Mohawk children of a minor box lacrosse team (Photo by Indian Time Newspaper)

A Mohawk nurse and a Mohawk pharmacist deliver services to the Akwesasne Community. (Photo by Indian Time Newspaper)

A Mohawk elder presents his garland of Onenhakenra, the traditional and ancient white corn of the Haudenosaunee.

Glossary

adder - a snake.
Aiionwatha (eye-en-thwah-tha) - the Mohawk word for Hiawatha. It means "He Who Combs."
alliance - a union of nations formed by agreement for some special purpose.
Atlantic whelk - a marine snail.
cattail - a slender reed that grows in the marsh.
clan - an extended family represented by an animal totem (symbol).
clan mother - an elder clan woman who keeps traditional teachings, advises people, holds the chiefs' titles, and selects new chiefs.
confederacy - a union of peoples joined together for a specific purpose.
cradleboard - a decorative flat board with a wooden band at the top that protects the baby's head.
faithkeeper - a spiritual advisor and keeper of traditional teachings. A faithkeeper also determines when ceremonies are to be held.
Great Law of Peace - a set of principles that teach how people should live in peace and harmony with each other and with the Natural World. It makes sure that the Natural World and the traditional teachings are preserved for future generations.
hide - an animal skin.
migrate - to go from one place to another with the change of seasons.
myth - a legend or story, usually one that tries to explain something in nature.
pelt - an animal skin with the fur still on it.
prophet - a person who tells that will happen.
quill - a stiff, sharp hair or spine.
rafter - a slanting beam of a roof.
reservation - tract of land set apart by a government for Native Americans to live on.
snare - a trap used to capture animals; often a loop of rope hung from a tree.
smoke hole - opening in the roof of the longhouse to allow smoke to go out.
symbol - something that stands for or represents something else.
tradition - the handing down of beliefs, customs, and stories from parents to children.
wampum - cylinder-shape beads made from Quahog and Atlantic Whelk. Wampum beads were woven into belts and strung on strings. It was used for ceremony, and as a form of barter and trade.
water drum - an Iroquois drum made from a hollowed out log. It is filled with water and covered with a leather hide.
woodland design - a design made of symbols representing vines, leaves, and flowers.

Web Sites

For general information about the Iroquois, see "Haudenosaunee Homework Help" at
www.peace4turtleisland.org For information on the National Museum of the American Indian,
see the Smithsonian's Web site at **www.si.edu/organiza/museums/amerind/abmus/index.htm**
For information on the Iroquois Indian Museum see **www.iroquoismuseum.org/**

These sites are subject to change. Go to your favorite search engine and type in "Iroquois" for more sites.

Index